The Good Samaritan

Luke 10: 25-37

RETOLD BY MARY BERENDES • ILLUSTRATED BY ROBERT SQUIER

Distributed by The Child's World®
1980 Lookout Drive • Mankato, MN 56003-1705
800-599-READ • www.childsworld.com

ACKNOWLEDGMENTS
The Child's World®: Mary Berendes, Publishing Director
The Design Lab: Art Direction and Design
Red Line Editorial: Contributing Editor
Natalie Mortensen: Contributing Editor

LIBRARY OF CONGRESS CATALOGING-IN-PUBLICATION DATA
Berendes, Mary.
  The Good Samaritan / by Mary Berendes; illustrated by Robert Squier.
    p. cm.
  ISBN 978-1-60954-391-4 (library reinforced: alk. paper)
  1. Good Samaritan (Parable)—Juvenile literature. 2. Bible stories, English—
N.T. Gospels—Juvenile literature. I. Squier, Robert, ill. II. Title.
  BT378.G6B47 2011
  226.8'09505—dc22   2011004955

Printed in the United States of America in Mankato, Minnesota.
July 2011
PA02087

The parables of the Bible are simple, easy-to-remember stories that Jesus told. Even though the stories are simple, they have deeper meanings.

esus was a smart man. Sometimes people tried to fool him. One day, a lawyer asked Jesus a question to trick him.

"Jesus," asked the lawyer, "what should I do to get into Heaven?"

"You are a lawyer," said Jesus. "You have studied the law. What is the rule?"

The lawyer thought a moment. Then he said, "You must love God with all your heart, and you must love your neighbor as you love yourself."

"Correct," said Jesus.

"But who is my neighbor?" asked the lawyer.

Jesus smiled. He told the lawyer this story to help him understand:

Once a man was traveling
from Jerusalem to Jericho.
The road he took was long
and lonely. It was also very
dangerous.

During his journey, the
man was attacked! Thieves
jumped upon him. They beat
him and kicked him. They
stole his money and clothes.

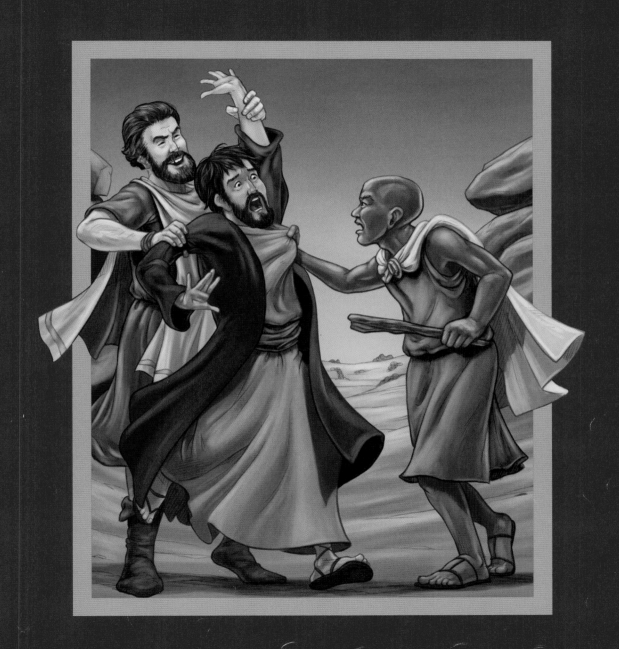

The thieves left the man by the side of the road. He was dirty and bleeding. He was badly hurt. He needed help.

Soon another traveler came by. But when he saw the wounded man, he went to the other side of the road. He hurried past. He did not want to help.

A short while later, another traveler came by. But as soon as he saw the wounded man, he also hurried by. He did not want to help, either.

Hours passed. Finally, another traveler came along. This man was a Samaritan—an enemy of the wounded man's people!

When the Samaritan saw
the wounded man, he felt
sorry for him. The Samaritan
stopped to help.

The Samaritan gently
cleaned the stranger's wounds
with wine and oil. He then
bandaged them with strips
of cloth.

He put the stranger on his
own donkey and took him
to the nearest inn. There he
cared for him all night.

"Now," said Jesus, "which
of these three men was the
true neighbor to the wounded
man?"

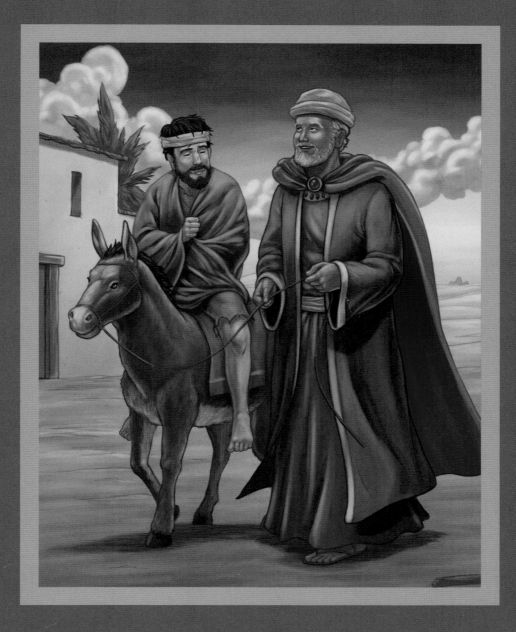

"The Samaritan," said the lawyer.

"Correct," said Jesus with a soft smile. "We should always try to treat other people just as the good Samaritan did."

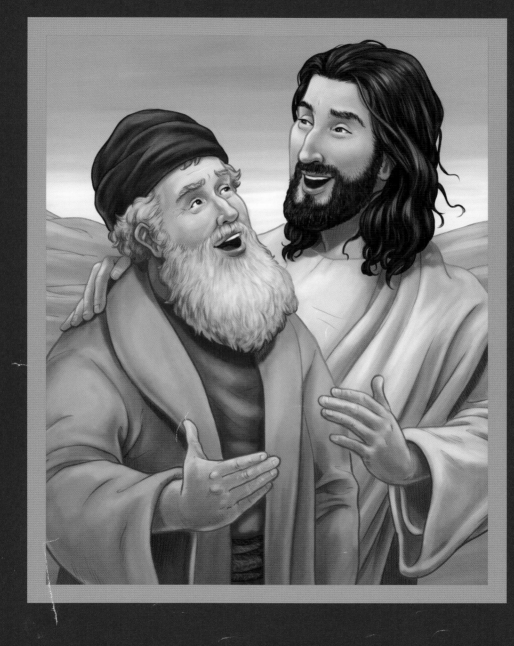

BEYOND THE STORY

In the parable of the good Samaritan, Jesus is trying to teach us what it means to really fulfill the idea of loving one's neighbor. During Jesus' time, the Samaritans were hated by the Jews. There was a very defined order to the people in society according to the Jewish community. This is important to know because it affected who they viewed as "neighbors," or people worthy of their help. There was the priest at the center, then the Levites or religious assistants. The Jewish people came next; further out were the tax collectors and thieves. The Samaritans were the farthest out in the circle. When the lawyer asked Jesus the question, "Who is my neighbor?" he is really asking how far out in the circle he has to go.

This story is believable because the road the Jew was traveling was very dangerous. Jesus never identifies the injured man but since his audience is Jewish they assume he is Jewish as well. The traveler is terribly wounded, left for dead, and needs help. Jesus helps the lawyer understand that the way you love people also shows your relationship with God. All of the people who go past the injured man leave him for different reasons. Only the Samaritan stops to care for his sworn enemy. He lives up to the real meaning behind the rule—to love your neighbor as you love yourself. The Samaritan teaches us that even our enemies are our neighbors and that every one is equal in the eyes of God no matter what group they belong to. He showed compassion by caring for the injured man. He even went so far as to give the innkeeper money to continue his care.

The parable helps us understand that we cannot put restrictions on who is deserving of our love. Like God, we must love everyone as we love ourselves.

Mary Berendes has authored dozens of books for children, including nature titles as well as books about countries and holidays. She loves to collect antique books and has some that are almost 200 years old. Mary lives in Minnesota.

Robert Squier has been drawing ever since he could hold a crayon. Today, instead of using crayons, he uses pencils, paint, and the computer. Robert lives in New Hampshire with his wife.